UNINTENTIONAL MENTORS

HOLD MY BEER

I'VE GOT A LESSON COMING

SETH CARPIEN

Copyright © 2025 by Seth Carpien
All rights reserved.

No part of this publication may be reproduced, stored in a retrieval system, or transmitted in any form or by any means—electronic, mechanical, photocopying, recording, or otherwise—without the prior written permission of the publisher, except for brief quotations used in reviews, articles, or scholarly works.

Published by **Atlas Elite Publishing Partners**
Cover design by **Michael Beas**

Paperback ISBN: 978-1-962825-88-7

Printed in United States of America

For more information, visit:
www.atlaselitepublishingpartners.com

Dedicated to my family—and to everyone who unintentionally made me wiser, funnier, or more confused. You know who you are.

TABLE OF CONTENTS

INTRODUCTION — 1

PART I THE EARLY LESSONS — 3

   CHAPTER 1 No Handouts — 5
   CHAPTER 2 Never Say Sorry — 9
   CHAPTER 3 Keep It Simple — 14
   CHAPTER 4 15 Seconds or Less — 18
   CHAPTER 5 Just a Puppet — 22
   CHAPTER 6 People vs. Money — 26
   CHAPTER 7 Company Man — 30

PART II THE GROWTH YEARS — 33

   CHAPTER 8 Football Coach — 35
   CHAPTER 9 Fixing Toilets — 39
   CHAPTER 10 Drop the Entitlement / Micro Management — 43
   CHAPTER 11 Loyalty Can Destroy — 47
   CHAPTER 12 I Know What I'm Doing — 51
   INTERLUDE Looking for a Career, Not a Job — 54

PART III TRANSFORMATION & LEADERSHIP — 57

   CHAPTER 13 Great to Blame — 59
   CHAPTER 14 Know When to Bring in the Cavalry — 64
   CHAPTER 15 Better Know Your Company Values — 68
   CHAPTER 16 WTF Am I Thinking! — 72
   CHAPTER 17 Micro What?! That's what she said… — 76
   CHAPTER 18 The Wolf in Khakis and an Oxford — 80

PART IV HONORING THE MENTORS — 84

CHAPTER 19 Homage to My Intentional Mentors — 86
CHAPTER 20 Unintentional Mentors I Never Met, But Hope To — 92
CHAPTER 21 What Is to Come — 97

BONUS CHAPTER THE 15 MINUTE MENTOR FRAMEWORK (YOURS FREE!) — 99

AUTHOR BIO — 102

INTRODUCTION

I'm not famous. No one's asking me to sign books at airports or give TED Talks about "crushing it." But once, someone said to me, "You really know who you want to be. I wish I did." That stuck with me — because it's true. It took longer than I'd like to admit, but I finally know who I want to be in my professional life. And more importantly, I know who I *don't* want to be.

That's what this book is about: the people who taught me both.

Most career advice books paint mentorship as this intentional, formal thing — the wise guru taking the eager protégé under their wing. That's not what happened to me. My mentors didn't even know they were mentoring me. Some inspired me by leading with vision, humility, and grit. Others? They taught me through sheer awfulness — showing me exactly how *not* to lead. They were unintentional mentors, every last one of them.

In this book, "Leaders" are the people who pushed me forward in positive ways — the ones who encouraged me, challenged me, and gave me space to grow. "Managers," on the other hand, are the ones who handed me cautionary tales — micromanagers, credit-stealers, screamers, the people whose example made me think, *Dear God, never let me become that.*

Funny thing is, they all shaped me. Every single stop along my career — from selling sneakers in high school to running teams in fintech and beyond — left fingerprints on who I am today as a leader. At the time, I didn't always notice. But looking back? Every bad boss, every clueless coworker, every genuine mentor added a piece to the puzzle.

Sometimes, the lessons were practical: how to cold-call without sounding like a robot, why you never say "sorry" when you actually mean "I won't do that again," or why you always keep extra pressed shirts in your trunk. Other times, the lessons were bigger: how to handle failure, how to check your ego, how to know when it's time to leave, and how to find work that doesn't make you miserable.

This isn't a "how-to" book. It's not "Ten Steps to Guaranteed Career Glory" (if you find that book, let me borrow it). It's a reflection — my unfiltered stories of the people who shaped me, for better or worse, and what I learned from them. My hope is that you'll see yourself in some of these stories: in the scrappy first job, the nightmare boss, the surprising mentor you didn't recognize until years later. And maybe it'll help you make sense of your own career — where you've been, where you're going, and who's unintentionally mentoring *you* right now.

Oh, and one more thing: this book goes in order of lessons, not chronology. Early on, the lessons were about me — figuring out what I wanted, where I fit, and how not to screw up every opportunity I was given. Later, the lessons shift to leading teams and shaping culture. That's how careers work: you start by surviving on your own, then you figure out how to help others survive (and hopefully thrive) too.

By the end, I hope you'll see what I eventually learned:

- Leadership isn't about titles.
- Mentorship doesn't always come with permission.
- And assholes make great teachers — if you know how to listen.

PART I
THE EARLY LESSONS

> Every story starts somewhere – mine began with gas money and a reality check.

CHAPTER 1
NO HANDOUTS

Lesson: Gas isn't free – neither is success.

My mom didn't believe in handouts. She believed in work. Real work. And she communicated that philosophy with the subtlety of a sledgehammer: "Gas isn't free in this house."

That was her way of saying, "Congrats on turning sixteen — now get a job." I wanted to spend my summer driving around with friends, wasting gas like it was infinite and free. She wanted me employed. Her reasoning was simple: if I was going to enjoy freedom, I had to earn it.

To understand her, you have to understand where she came from. My mom grew up in Reading, Pennsylvania — one of eight kids packed into a small row house. When she told me stories about her childhood, I pictured something between *The Grapes of Wrath* and a Catholic school field trip. Homemade bread, hand-me-down everything, and yes, reused toilet paper. (I never asked for details.) That kind of upbringing leaves an impression. By the time she had kids, she and my dad were doing well, but she made sure my sister and I understood what "earning it" meant.

So, there I was: sixteen, broke, desperate for gas money, and tasked with finding a job. My first attempt? Fast food. I lasted one day. The Saturday lunch rush nearly broke me — grease popping, people shouting, my brown visor absorbing sweat like a sponge. By the end of my shift, I smelled like a deep fryer and decided I would do anything — anything — to find something better.

This was pre-internet. No Indeed, no LinkedIn, no "Easy Apply" button. You either walked into stores to beg for applications or you cold-called. I chose cold-calling. I sat in my friend's basement with a phone book — yes, an actual paper phone book — and dialed every retail store I could think of. Clothing stores, record shops, sporting goods. Most calls ended the same way:

"Hi, I'm looking for a summer job."

"We're not hiring." Click.

But I kept calling. Stubbornness has always been one of my better qualities.

Finally, I struck gold: Foot Locker. "Come in and fill out an application," the guy said. Victory. I landed my first "cool" job.

Selling sneakers in the late '80s was about as cool as it got for a city kid. This was peak Air Jordan era — sneakers were currency. Kids lined up for releases, and working at Foot Locker felt like being backstage at a rock concert. Sure, the uniform was a polyester referee outfit that made me look like a knockoff NFL official, but at least it didn't smell like fryer grease.

The job itself was pure sales. I learned how to talk to people, figure out what they wanted, and help them find it. I learned how to upsell — "You're getting Jordans? You're going to want socks and cleaner too." And I learned something about myself: I was good at it. I liked talking to people. I liked solving problems. I liked walking someone to the register knowing I'd made their day (and boosted my commission).

At the time, I didn't think of my mom as a mentor. She wasn't sitting me down for life lessons or walking me through career options. She just wanted me out of the house and paying for my own gas. But years later, looking back, I realized she taught me something fundamental: you don't wait for opportunities — you go find them.

LESSON LEARNED

The lesson wasn't just "get a job" — it was bigger than that. My mom didn't hand me anything because she knew life wouldn't either. The summer I got that first job, I learned that opportunities rarely knock; you have to go banging on doors (or, in my case, calling every store in the phone book) until one opens. And when it does, you better be ready to work for it.

Years later, I still carry that mindset. Promotions, new roles, big projects — none of them fell into my lap. I had to ask. I had to prove I deserved them. And while it would've been nice to have things handed to me, earning them felt better. That's the thing about hard-earned opportunities: they stick with you, and they shape how you lead others. Today, I tell my teams the same thing my mom told me — maybe with less bluntness about gas money, but the point stands: no handouts.

> Some lessons hit you gently.
> Others yell at you from across the bar.

CHAPTER 2
NEVER SAY SORRY

Lesson: "Sorry" is cheap; fix it instead.

The first time I met Butch McGuire — yes, *that* Butch McGuire — I was fresh out of college, broke, and desperate. I had no job lined up after graduation, no savings, and no real plan beyond "move to Chicago and figure it out." Not exactly a strategic career path, but I was twenty-two and convinced the world owed me something just for showing up with a diploma.

Chicago, for the record, didn't care.

After two months of sleeping on a friend's couch and pretending I had things "lined up," I finally admitted I needed work. Any work. So, one afternoon, I wandered down Division Street, walking into every bar I passed, asking if they were hiring. Some laughed, some ignored me, but then I stepped into Butch McGuire's.

It was like walking into another world. The place was legendary — dark wood walls, Christmas lights strung up year-round, a bar that stretched forever, and the faint smell of beer-soaked history. In the back, sitting at a table like some kind of cigar-chomping godfather, was Butch himself.

"What do you want, kid?" he barked without looking up.

"Uh... I'm looking for a job," I said.

"What kind of job?"

"Whatever you need me to do."

That sealed it. No résumé, no interview. Just "come back at five with a pressed white shirt." That was my introduction to Butch — short, blunt, and somehow exactly what I needed.

Now, I didn't own a white shirt. And I definitely didn't own an iron. So I did what any resourceful broke twenty-something would do: hit up a thrift store. I found something vaguely white and ironed it until I thought it looked decent. When I showed up early for my first shift, proud of my effort, Butch took one look at me and said, "That shirt isn't pressed. Go change."

"Sorry," I muttered automatically.

Big mistake.

Butch wheeled on me, cigar wagging, voice booming over the bar noise.

"Don't say sorry. Don't EVER say sorry."

It wouldn't be the last time I heard it.

Working at Butch's was chaos — long shifts, endless crowds, Irish music blaring, orders flying in from every direction. Butch ran the place like a football coach: loud, demanding, relentless. He yelled a lot. But there was a method to it. He cared about the details — the way drinks were poured, how tables were bussed, how the staff looked. He believed in doing things right, and if you couldn't handle the heat, you didn't last.

And me? I said "sorry" a lot. Every time I made a mistake, every time I fumbled an order, every time Butch barked at me, "sorry" slipped out. And every single time, he shut me down.

"Don't say sorry!"

"What did I JUST say about sorry?"

"If you say sorry one more time, you're out of here!"

At first, I thought he was just being an asshole. But over time, I realized what he was teaching me. Butch didn't hate humility — he hated empty apologies. "Sorry" is easy. It's a reflex. It's what you say when you want someone to stop being mad at you, not when you're actually taking responsibility. Butch wanted ownership. He wanted acknowledgment.

There's a huge difference between "sorry" and "I screwed that up — won't happen again." One is noise. The other is accountability.

By the time I left Butch's six months later, I had learned how to work hard, how to handle chaos, and how to own my mistakes without groveling. I'd also learned how to iron, which turned out to be a surprisingly useful life skill.

Butch died years later, and when I heard the news, I cried a little. Not because we were close — we weren't — but because he mattered. He was one of my first unintentional mentors. The guy who yelled at me taught me more about leadership (and humility) than most people who tried to "coach" me nicely. And I'll never forget him for it.

LESSON LEARNED

Butch's constant "don't say sorry" wasn't about banning apologies. It was about forcing accountability. "Sorry" is easy — it's a reflex, something you throw out so people stop being mad. Owning the mistake is harder. It requires you to name what went wrong, fix it, and not do it again.

In leadership, I've seen the difference firsthand. Teams trust leaders who admit mistakes, not ones who constantly say "sorry" and repeat them. And I've learned to look for that same accountability in others. If someone messes up and says, "I'll fix it," I know they're learning. If all I hear is "sorry," I know I'll be having the same conversation again in a week. Butch might've been rough around the edges, but he ingrained in me something I still practice daily: acknowledgment over apology.

> Success doesn't always show up in a suit – sometimes it smells like motor oil.

CHAPTER 3
KEEP IT SIMPLE

Lesson: Confuse them, lose them – keep it simple.

I've said this before and I'll say it again: Victor Malloy was the best salesperson I've ever met. He could sell anything to anyone — commodities, cars, probably even a screen door to a submarine. The man had a gift. He was also, let's be honest, probably skating a fine line between "savvy entrepreneur" and "future FBI case study." But I'll get to that.

I first met Victor at a fraternity homecoming event. I'd graduated a year earlier, but like most recent grads, I wasn't quite ready to let go of college life. So there I was, back at my alma mater, reliving the glory days — cheap beer, bad decisions, no real responsibilities. Amid the chaos of kegs and nostalgia walks in this guy: older, sharp suit, perfect hair, and a presence that just screamed I've made it. He introduced himself as an alum from the '70s. We started talking, and within minutes he had me thinking about my future — something I had been actively avoiding up until that moment.

Victor lived in Chicago and ran a commodities trading firm. He told me about his business, his clients, the kind of success he was having, and most importantly, the lifestyle — nice suits, fancy dinners, motorcycles, the whole nine yards. I'd been working at Butch McGuire's, barely scraping by, so you can imagine how appealing this sounded. Victor painted the picture so well I could practically see myself in that Armani suit (spoiler: I never got one).

A few weeks later, I took him up on the offer and joined his firm. That's when I realized two things:

1. Victor really was the best salesperson I'd ever met.
2. The company looked nothing like the dream he sold me.

The office was over a car repair shop in Rogers Park — and not the cool, gentrified Rogers Park of today. We're talking 1990s Rogers Park, where you locked your car doors twice and prayed the El showed up on time. The "trading floor" was basically a cramped room with desks jammed together, phones everywhere, and sales scripts taped to the walls. This wasn't Wall Street. This was *Boiler Room* before *Boiler Room* was even a movie.

The job was simple: 300 cold calls a day. Three hundred. We didn't have headsets — those were too expensive — so we used these ridiculous shoulder harnesses that dug into your neck after about ten calls. I'd leave every day with a stiff neck, a raw ear, and a strong desire to quit. But here's the crazy part: I didn't. I stuck with it. And I got good.

Victor's whole philosophy was simplicity. He drilled it into us from day one: don't overcomplicate, don't overexplain. Clients don't want a lecture; they want solutions. Figure out what they need, explain it clearly, and stop talking. The second you start rambling, you lose them.

We practiced this relentlessly. Scripts, role-playing, objections — not that kind of role-playing, you sicko — until it felt natural. And it worked. I went from struggling to close a deal to leading the board in just a few months. The formula was simple: say what matters, nothing more.

And then things got... interesting.

There were whispers about some of the deals Victor was doing. Rumors of "creative" accounting. And then, one day, the FBI showed up. (Yep. That happened.) I never found out the full story — and honestly, I didn't want to. Shortly after, Victor was out of the industry, and I was looking for another job. Not exactly the career launch I'd envisioned when I first shook his hand at homecoming.

But here's the thing: I don't regret it. Because buried under all the chaos and questionable ethics was a lesson I still use today: keep it simple. In sales, in leadership, even in life — simplicity wins. Overcomplicating loses people. The best pitch, the best strategy, the best idea is the one you can explain clearly and quickly. Anything more is just noise.

LESSON LEARNED

Victor may have had questionable ethics, but his approach to communication was bulletproof: keep it simple. I didn't realize it then, but that skill would become one of the most valuable in my career. Whether you're selling sneakers, pitching a strategy to your boss, or leading a team through change, clarity wins. People tune out the second you drown them in details they don't need.

Over the years, I've learned to strip messages down to their core. What problem are we solving? What's the solution? Why does it matter? That's it. Ironically, it's often harder to make something simple than to make it complicated. But when you can take a mess of information and distill it into something clear, people listen — and they trust you. That's the difference between noise and influence.

> The smartest people don't always talk the longest – and neither should you.

CHAPTER 4
15 SECONDS OR LESS

Lesson: If you need a TED Talk, you've already lost them.

When I finally left Chicago, I thought I was moving on to something bigger, cleaner, and more professional. No more yelling bosses in bars, no more shoulder harnesses digging into my neck while I dialed 300 cold calls a day, and — hopefully — no more surprise FBI visits. I moved back to D.C., where I grew up, and landed a job at a financial services firm as an assistant to a team of advisors.

The idea was simple: get my foot in the door, learn the ropes, and eventually get my licenses so I could become an advisor myself. It felt like a smart next step. Steady job, steady pay, and, in my mind, a stepping stone toward the "real career" I was supposed to be building. What I didn't realize was that my next big lesson in leadership was waiting for me in the form of Suzy McGovern.

Suzy was the compliance officer. If you've never worked in financial services, compliance is basically the person who makes sure nobody is breaking the law — which is important, because in that industry, people are always about two bad decisions away from breaking the law. Suzy's job was to review trades, approve accounts, and keep the entire office from stepping over the line. She also oversaw all the assistants, which meant she was technically my boss.

Suzy was one of the toughest people I've ever worked with — and I mean that as a compliment. She didn't take crap from anyone, which in the mid-

'90s financial world was no small feat. The place was still very much a boys' club, and Suzy had carved out her authority the hard way: by being smarter, faster, and sharper than everyone else in the room. She wasn't loud, but she didn't need to be. People respected her because she got things done.

She also didn't tolerate inefficiency. At all.

I learned this the hard way my first week on the job. I had a question about a form — something small, probably something I should've figured out myself — and I hovered in her doorway waiting for her to notice me. When she did, I started rambling. I didn't have my thoughts organized. I didn't know exactly what I was asking. I was basically just hoping she'd fix it for me. She let me get about ten seconds in before she cut me off.

"If you can't ask me in fifteen seconds," she said, "come back when you can."

And then she went right back to her work.

I stood there stunned. Fifteen seconds? That's all I get? But over time, I realized she was right. Hovering in someone's doorway, talking in circles, wasting their time — it wasn't just annoying, it was unproductive. If I couldn't explain what I needed in fifteen seconds, I wasn't prepared to ask the question in the first place.

So I adapted. Before I went to Suzy, I got my thoughts straight. I rehearsed my ask in my head. I made sure I had all the information I needed so I could get right to the point. Over time, it became second nature — not just with Suzy, but with everyone. It forced me to cut the fluff, focus on what mattered, and respect people's time.

And here's the thing: people *love* it when you respect their time. When you get to the point fast, they're more likely to listen, more likely to help, and more likely to trust you. Suzy's fifteen-second rule didn't just make me better at my job; it made me better at communicating in general. Even today, I'll catch myself mid-sentence, stop, back up, and say, "Let me try that again." It's Suzy's voice in my head, and it works every time.

Outside of work, Suzy was just as memorable. She had this incredible mix of toughness and humor, the kind of person who could cut someone down to size in one breath and make you laugh in the next. She even gave me what I still consider the most insane tanning advice I've ever heard: "Day one, 40 SPF. Day two, 30. Day three, 20. Day four? Straight oil." (For legal reasons, I am not endorsing this plan, but Suzy always came back from vacation with the perfect tan, so who am I to argue?)

Over the years, Suzy became more than just my boss; she became a friend. She even gave me "Assistant of the Year" in my second year — the only award I've ever won with "of the Year" in the title. After I left, we stayed in touch. Last I heard, she'd moved on to work for one of the governing bodies of the financial industry — which makes sense, because if anyone was going to keep the rest of us honest, it was Suzy.

LESSON LEARNED

Suzy's "fifteen-second rule" changed more than just how I asked her questions — it changed how I communicate, period. In business, time is currency. The faster you can get to the point, the more respect you earn. People don't remember how long you talked; they remember whether you said something worth hearing.

This applies whether you're in a one-on-one, pitching to a client, or speaking to an entire team. The best communicators prepare, cut the fluff, and say what matters. Suzy didn't sugarcoat it, but she was right: if you can't explain it in fifteen seconds, you're not ready to talk about it. That's a skill I use every day — and one I try to pass on to my teams.

> Not every bad boss is useless – some accidentally show you the right way forward.

CHAPTER 5
JUST A PUPPET

Lesson: Don't be the boss's pet parrot.

By the time I left the firm where I'd worked with Suzy McGovern, I thought I had leadership figured out. Suzy had shown me what good management looked like — direct, fair, efficient. She set high standards, but she supported you. She called you out, but she also had your back. I figured, *Okay, this is what it's supposed to be like. Wherever I go next, it'll be the same.*

Wrong.

My next stop was another financial services company. Bigger office, bigger client list, seemingly bigger opportunity. The team I joined was part of a high-performing group within the firm, almost like a business within the business. On paper, it looked like a great move. In reality, I had just walked into a masterclass on what not to do.

The group was led by a woman named Gloria Powerston. Gloria was a powerhouse — she had built the team from the ground up, brought in massive clients, and basically ran the show. Everyone in the office knew Gloria was the real decision-maker. The company might've had a formal org chart, but in practice, Gloria was the top of the food chain.

Enter Denise Peppersnapp, Gloria's right hand. Technically, Denise was the branch manager for our group — which meant she was supposed to oversee the day-to-day operations, keep things running smoothly, and manage the rest of us. In reality? She was Gloria's enforcer. Whatever

Gloria wanted, Denise made happen. No questions asked, no pushback, no independent thought. She was a "yes" person in the purest form.

At first, I didn't think much of it. Lots of managers play politics, right? But the longer I worked there, the clearer it became: Denise wasn't leading anyone. She wasn't protecting her team, she wasn't advocating for us, and she sure as hell wasn't making the office a better place to work. She spent her days carrying out Gloria's orders and nitpicking everyone else to prove she was "in charge."

The nitpicking was constant. Tiny, pointless things — how you stapled a document, where you left your coffee cup, the tone of an email. Meanwhile, the actual performers — the top producers who brought in the big accounts — ignored her completely. They didn't have to listen to her because their numbers spoke louder than any reprimand she could deliver. And because I worked closely with one of those top producers — my mom, as you'll learn in the next chapter — I got caught in the crossfire.

Denise didn't like that my mom ignored her. And by extension, she didn't like me either. She couldn't control my mom, but she could try to control me — and she did. Every little mistake I made, every minor oversight, Denise was there, wagging her proverbial finger. It wasn't leadership. It was theater. She didn't want to make me better; she wanted to make herself feel bigger.

It didn't take long for me to realize that Denise wasn't going to teach me anything about how to be a leader. But she was going to teach me something just as valuable: how not to be one.

Watching her, I saw what happens when you build your entire management style around pleasing the person above you instead of supporting the people below you. You lose trust. You lose respect. And eventually, you lose influence — because no one follows a puppet.

Years later, when I moved into leadership roles myself, I found myself thinking about Denise more than I'd like to admit. Any time I was tempted to blindly follow orders or micromanage my team, I'd remember how miserable it felt to be on the receiving end of that. And I'd ask myself: *Am I protecting my team right now, or am I just protecting myself?* That question has saved me more than once.

LESSON LEARNED

Denise was one of my first "anti-mentors." She didn't teach me how to lead; she showed me exactly how not to lead. Watching her blindly say "yes" to everything from above while micromanaging everyone below her was like a slow-motion train wreck. It made me realize something critical: leadership is a balancing act.

Good leaders protect their teams from unnecessary chaos. Great leaders also have the courage to push back when those above them are wrong. Puppets do neither. They follow orders, spread fear, and burn out the people around them. I never wanted to be that kind of leader. And every time I've had to stand up for my team — even when it's uncomfortable — I think back to Denise and remind myself why it matters.

> Chasing someone else's dream can teach you a lot about your own.

CHAPTER 6
PEOPLE VS. MONEY

Lesson: Love the work, not just the paycheck.

I've mentioned my mom a few times already — usually with some combination of admiration and sarcasm. But here's the thing: she wasn't just my mom; she was also one of the toughest, smartest financial advisors I've ever known. And for a brief (and wildly complicated) period, she was also my boss.

This was late '90s, early 2000s. I'd already bounced around a few sales roles, bartended at legendary bars, survived a borderline-shady commodities firm, and worked as an assistant at another financial services company. When I joined my mom's firm, I was finally a Certified Sales Assistant — licensed to trade, talk to clients, and do actual advisor work. And I thought, "Hey, maybe this is it. Maybe I take over my mom's book someday, keep it in the family." That idea lasted about... six months.

Let me back up. My mom — Jannet — grew up poor. One of eight kids in Reading, Pennsylvania, raised Catholic, which is basically a double major in guilt and frugality. She entered the financial industry in the 1970s, back when women weren't just underrepresented — they were actively pushed out. She survived by being smarter, sharper, and tougher than the guys around her. And by "tough," I don't mean loud or brash. I mean unflinching. She didn't put up with any crap, from anyone, ever.

The stories she'd tell me were insane. Like the time she was sitting in the bullpen making cold calls and the guys decided to celebrate a colleague's birthday by hiring strippers — in the middle of the office. In front of everyone. No one batted an eye. So on her birthday? She brought in a male stripper. Management freaked out. She basically said, "If I have to sit here through your circus, you can sit through mine." Guess what? The strippers stopped after that. That's my mom in a nutshell: fight fire with fire, and don't apologize.

By the time I joined her team, she had built a massive book of business — over $100 million under management. And she did it the hard way: researching companies herself, finding hidden opportunities, building long-term relationships. While other advisors were chasing the next hot stock, she was looking at the companies supplying those companies — the ones no one else was paying attention to. It was brilliant. It was also... not me.

I figured this out fast. My mom loved the research side — the spreadsheets, the market analysis, the deep dives into quarterly reports. I loved people. Relationships. Talking to clients, building trust, helping them feel good about where their money was going. In other words, she loved the *money* side. I loved the *people* side.

At first, I tried to force it. I told myself I could learn to love the analysis if I just pushed through. But every time I found myself staring at another earnings report, I felt my brain shutting off. Meanwhile, when I was on the phone with clients, I felt alive. I realized something important: this wasn't just a mismatch of skills — it was a mismatch of *interests*. And no amount of hard work fixes that.

Making it more complicated, working for your mom is... weird. There's no separating personal and professional. Every disagreement feels like five arguments rolled into one: boss vs. employee, mom vs. son, mentor vs. mentee, "I raised you better than this," and "why don't you listen to me?" all wrapped together. We butted heads constantly — about clients, about process, about where my career was headed. I think she wanted me to take over her book, but deep down, I think we both knew it wasn't the right fit.

Eventually, I left. Not because I didn't respect her — I did, deeply — but because I realized something important about myself: I didn't want her job. I didn't want her life. And that was okay.

It took me years to fully appreciate the lesson. At the time, I just felt guilty — like I'd failed her somehow. But looking back, I see it differently. My mom's career taught me what greatness looks like. It also taught me what doesn't fit me — which is just as valuable. Not every mentor shows you what you *should* be. Some show you what you *shouldn't*.

LESSON LEARNED

Working with my mom taught me something I didn't expect: just because someone is great at what they do doesn't mean you should follow their exact path. My mom loved the research, the analysis, the hunt for the next hidden gem in the markets. I didn't. I loved people — building relationships, earning trust, helping clients feel secure. We were both good at different things, and that's okay.

Too often, we chase roles that look impressive on paper instead of ones that fit who we are. That's a recipe for burnout. The real key is figuring out where your skills and your interests overlap — because that's where you'll thrive. My mom showed me that, even if she didn't mean to. Her success gave me permission to define my own.

> Sometimes loyalty looks like success – until you see the bill it leaves behind.

CHAPTER 7
COMPANY MAN

Lesson: If the company wins but the client loses, you've already lost.

By the time I landed at Cromwell & Chase, I thought I had this whole financial services thing figured out. I'd been an assistant, I'd done cold calls, I'd worked for my mom (survived that), and I'd convinced myself that an MBA would make everything make sense. Spoiler: it didn't.

I moved to Winston-Salem for the MBA program at Wake Forest, mostly because I needed to reset. My first year there was… not great. Let's just say I spent more time improving my golf game than my GPA. By the end of that year, I was on academic probation and desperately needed to prove I belonged. My brilliant idea? Get a job during the day, go to school at night, and claw my way back into respectability.

That's how I wound up as a junior partner at Cromwell & Chase, working in institutional sales under Bradley Shinyford.

Bradley was one of those guys who looked the part: sharp suits, perfect hair, confident stride. He ran the institutional side of the branch — the "grown-up" sales team dealing with big corporate accounts, not individual investors. And on paper, he was a perfect mentor: senior partner, branch manager, a guy who knew the business inside and out.

In reality? Bradley was the quintessential company man.

If you've never met one, here's the type: everything he did was for the good of the firm — not the client, not the team, not even himself (though the bonuses didn't hurt). He lived and breathed the company line. If the higher-ups said, "Push this product," Bradley pushed it, no questions asked. If the branch needed to make quota on some proprietary fund, Bradley treated it like gospel. Ethics? Client fit? Logic? Details. The company wanted it done, and Bradley was gonna do it.

The clearest example of this came during an IPO we were handling. The company — I'll call it Across the Water, or ATW (not its real name, but you get the idea) — was going public, and the firm had a huge allocation to sell. The deal was... questionable. Not outright fraudulent (this wasn't Enron), but shaky enough that any sane person would've hesitated before pushing it to clients. Not Bradley. Bradley didn't hesitate for a second.

The day before the IPO, Bradley handed me a list of clients and said, "Sell them 400 shares each. Don't ask questions." I barely knew anything about ATW. Hell, I barely knew what they did. So I asked Bradley, "Can you give me three reasons why this is a good buy? Just so I have something to tell them?" Bradley looked at me like I'd just asked him to solve quantum physics.

"They've got good financials," he said. "They're... good. Just sell it."

That was Bradley in a nutshell: do what the company needs, don't overthink it, move on to the next thing. And honestly? For a while, I played along. I wanted to prove myself. I wanted to be a team player. I wanted back into the MBA program, and having Bradley on my side didn't hurt.

But deep down, it didn't sit right. The clients weren't getting what they needed. They were getting what the company wanted them to buy. And when PATW tanked — which it eventually did — I realized just how dangerous that mindset could be.

Bradley wasn't a bad guy. He was smart, charismatic, and successful. But he taught me something I never forgot: loyalty to a company means nothing if it comes at the expense of the people you serve.

LESSON LEARNED

Bradley Shinyford taught me one of the hardest lessons of my career: loyalty to a company means nothing if it comes at the expense of your clients. Bradley's priority was always the firm — quotas, initiatives, whatever the higher-ups wanted. Clients came second. And when the deals went bad, the clients were the ones left holding the bag.

That stuck with me. No matter what company I've worked for, I've always believed my first obligation is to the people I serve — clients, customers, my team. Companies change. Leaders come and go. But the relationships you build — the trust you earn — that's what lasts. Bradley didn't mean to teach me that lesson, but I'm grateful he did. It's shaped every decision I've made since.

PART II
THE GROWTH YEARS

> Not every coach knows the game they're screaming about.

CHAPTER 8
FOOTBALL COACH

*Lesson: You can lead like a coach, or you can scream like one.
One of those builds a team.*

If you've ever watched a college football coach on the sidelines losing their damn mind over a missed block — red in the face, headset flying off, spit particles hitting the backup punter — you've already met Dan Carmichael.

Except Dan wasn't on a football field. He was my office manager.

I was a young Financial Advisor in training, which meant I was on the phone all day trying to convince people to trust me with their life savings while still paying off a Target credit card in monthly installments. Meanwhile, Dan's job was to "support" me — at least on paper. In reality, he was the guy screaming from the sidelines, clipboard in hand, yelling about numbers, performance, and how someone else was always doing it better.

He liked to call himself a coach. But Dan wasn't coaching. He was berating. He thought motivation came from threats, not trust. Inspiration, in his mind, was just a louder volume setting on a microphone no one asked for.

I'll never forget the time he stood up in the middle of the bullpen and shouted, "If you're not making a hundred dials a day, you might as well pack it in now!" Like that was going to light a fire under us. One guy actually did pack it in and walked out with his headset still around his neck. I never saw him again. Legend.

Dan's style was all bark, more bark, and then maybe a random passive-aggressive comment just to keep things spicy. He wanted us to fear him, not respect him. He confused activity with productivity and treated every missed opportunity like it was a dropped touchdown pass in the fourth quarter.

To be clear — I was successful in spite of Dan, not because of him. I made my calls, built real relationships, and hustled because I had internal drive, not because someone was screaming over my shoulder like we were down by seven with two minutes left.

The irony is, Dan thought he was building a team. What he was really doing was exhausting one. You ever try to perform at your best with someone breathing down your neck like a CrossFit instructor with anger issues? Yeah, not optimal. Turns out shame and panic don't make great performance metrics.

The best part? When I finally started to hit my stride — building a real book of business, getting calls returned, seeing clients stick with me — Dan took credit. "See? That's how coaching works!"
No, Dan. That's how not listening to you works.

LESSON LEARNED

Leadership is not yelling. It's not threatening. And it's definitely not taking credit for someone else's grit. Coach Dan thought he was a football coach, but in reality, he was just a guy with a clipboard and a complex. He mistook volume for value and control for respect.

The best leaders don't scream at you to perform — they show you how. They step into the work, not onto a soapbox. Dan did none of that. But I'll give him credit for one thing: he showed me exactly the kind of "coach" I never wanted to be.

So next time you think yelling is the answer, ask yourself — are you coaching, or just making noise? Dan chose noise. I chose better.

> From external mentors
> (and anti-mentors) to internal growth.

CHAPTER 9
FIXING TOILETS

Lesson: Sometimes the person you need to learn from is standing in your shoes – preferably not while the toilet's overflowing.

There's a moment in every person's life when they look in the mirror and think:

"How the hell did I end up here... elbow-deep in toilet water?"

For me, that moment came when I owned a restaurant. That's right, a full-on, doors-open, food-served, taxes-paid (well, eventually) restaurant. I wasn't just managing the place — I *owned* it. It was my name on the paperwork, my money in the bank account (or not in the bank account, depending on the week), and my responsibility when shit broke. Literally.

Now, when people hear you own a restaurant, they assume it's glamorous. Cocktails, curated menus, hip lighting, maybe a little jazz in the background. Let me clear that up: restaurant ownership is basically just firefighting in an apron. One day you're reprinting menus because the chef decided to "experiment" with an all-beet pasta night, and the next you're crawling on the floor of the men's bathroom because a customer decided to treat the toilet like a trash compactor.

This particular day, the toilet stopped flushing. I don't mean it was *clogged* — I mean it gave up. Like it had seen too much and said, "No more."

There was no plumber in sight, and no one on staff knew what to do except stare at it like it might fix itself out of guilt. So I did the only thing I could do: I Googled "how to fix a commercial toilet," rolled up my sleeves (after changing shirts — I'm not a savage), and got to work.

Two hours later — after a lot of grunting, sweating, and one unfortunate moment involving a wrench and a faceful of tank water — I fixed the damn thing. The toilet flushed. I stood there in soaked jeans, victorious, like some weird plumbing-themed Rocky Balboa. I think Eye of the Tiger played in my head. The staff clapped. Or maybe they were just relieved the bathroom reopened. Either way, it felt good.

But here's what mattered: I learned something that day. Not just how to fix a toilet, but that I could teach myself whatever the hell I needed to learn. I didn't need someone holding my hand. I didn't need permission. I just needed a problem, a little time, and the willingness to look stupid until I figured it out.

I was my own mentor that day. And you know what? I crushed it.

LESSON LEARNED

When you become a leader, you also become a student — again and again. And sometimes the best teacher is you, in the middle of a mess, figuring it out as you go. That toilet didn't care that I was the owner. And life doesn't care about your title when the shit hits the fan — pun very much intended.

The real takeaway? Your team notices when you're willing to get dirty. When you show you'll do the work, you earn respect — not because you demanded it, but because you modeled it. That said, there's a line. Just because you *can* fix the toilet doesn't mean you *should* every time. True leadership is about knowing when to dive in — and when to step back and let others own it.

So yeah, I fixed a toilet. And in the process, I fixed a little part of myself too: the part that thought leadership was about delegating from a safe distance.

Turns out sometimes the best kind of management... is plumbing.

A villain in your mind, only to become an unintentional mentor.

CHAPTER 10
DROP THE ENTITLEMENT / MICRO MANAGEMENT

Lesson: Sometimes the jerk in the room is you.

There was a time in my career when I thought I was *the guy*. I was a Regional Sales Manager at a B2B magazine in the early 2000s — which, back then, was still a thing. Digital hadn't eaten the whole world yet, and print ads still had power. And I was good at selling them. Like, *really* good.

I had swagger, numbers to back it up, and more confidence than a 23-year-old with frosted tips and a Bluetooth headset. I thought I was the next big thing in media. The Don Draper of trade publications, minus the whiskey in the morning. (Most days.)

Then came Bruce Shulman.

Bruce was my manager. His job, apparently, was to make mine miserable — at least that's what I told myself at the time. He micromanaged every move I made. "Did you log that call?" "What's your plan for next week?" "Why didn't you include the northeast client list in that report?" "Are you wearing that shirt on purpose?"

It felt like he was breathing down my neck every damn day. I remember thinking: *This guy must be insecure. Or power hungry. Or both.* Meanwhile, I was just trying to crush deals and collect checks. Let me sell, Bruce. I don't need a babysitter.

Or so I thought.

About two years into working together — after countless tension-filled meetings, a few passive-aggressive emails, and several hallway stare-downs — something shifted.

Bruce invited me out for drinks one night. Now, let me pause and say that Bruce didn't *look* like the "grab-a-drink-and-shoot-the-shit" type. He looked like he should be managing a New Jersey deli and yelling at you for how you ordered your sandwich. But that night, he suggested we grab a beer and "check out the local entertainment." I won't get into details, but let's just say it wasn't a poetry reading.

I went, mostly because I was curious what Bruce was like outside of work. What I found was a completely different guy. Funny. Relaxed. Knew everyone in town. And for the first time, we had an actual conversation — not about forecasts or ad impressions, but about me, my future, and *why* he'd been on me so much.

Turns out, I had been an entitled little shit when I joined. (His words? No. But the subtext was there.) I had come in swinging like I deserved the world just because I was hitting quota. But I wasn't doing the *full job*. And more than that, Bruce wasn't micromanaging me out of ego — he was *protecting* me. His boss, the big boss, thought I wasn't pulling my weight and wanted me gone. Bruce was shielding me from the fallout and trying to steer me in the right direction. He just didn't say it with hugs and compliments. He said it with spreadsheets and deadlines.

That night changed everything. Not because Bruce stopped managing me the same way — but because *I* started seeing it differently. I realized I wasn't the misunderstood prodigy. I was the rookie who had a lot to learn — about work ethic, about humility, and about what it really means to earn your spot.

And Bruce? He became one of the most important unintentional mentors in my career.

We still talk to this day. Mostly about family, sports, and how I used to be a pain in the ass. Which I was. But hey — we grow.

LESSON LEARNED

Entitlement is a career killer — and it's especially dangerous because you rarely see it in yourself. I thought Bruce was the micromanaging villain in my story, but I was the one making it hard. I expected trust without accountability. I expected praise without putting in the extra work. I thought results alone made me bulletproof.

Bruce taught me that being good at your job isn't the same as being *great* at it. And leadership isn't always about being liked — sometimes it's about protecting people from themselves and holding them to a higher standard, even if they don't get it at the time.

So the next time your boss is "riding you," pause before you label them the problem. Ask yourself: "Am I really doing the job? Or am I just doing the parts I like and expecting applause?"

Thanks, Bruce — for being the jerk I needed to learn from.

(And for that one unforgettable night in town... even if we never speak of it again.)

> "Loyalty versus leadership".
> What happens when a leader
> fails to act.

CHAPTER 11
LOYALTY CAN DESTROY

Lesson: Loyalty is noble – until it becomes negligence.

I should've known better the moment I left a perfectly good sales job to chase the startup dream. But there was something about Jason Fairchild that pulled me in. He was sharp, driven, and had that "future CEO of something big" energy. Think Steve Jobs, if Jobs wore Dockers and said "awesome" a lot.

This was the mid-2000s, when fintech was still finding its legs. The company Jason co-founded had built a sleek new financial planning platform — and at the time, it felt revolutionary. I mean, most advisors were still faxing things back then. We were going to drag the industry into the 21st century with clean UI, smart workflows, and some wild thing called "cloud-based access." Oooooh.

Jason brought me in to run sales. It felt like a dream gig — lean team, cool product, huge upside. And then there was Trevor Smoke. Jason's co-founder. The guy who supposedly had the keys to the kingdom.

Trevor was... intense. You know that guy in the meeting who says things like "we're about to explode" and "we're talking to [insert tech giant here] about a massive deal"? That was Trevor — except he wasn't exaggerating. He was lying. Boldly. Constantly. With a straight face and no soul behind the eyes.

When I joined, Trevor told me he had dozens of prospects lined up — warm leads, ready to close. All I had to do was swoop in, dazzle them with the demo, and rake in the deals. Easy money, right? Wrong. I started calling these "leads" and got a whole lot of "Trevor who?" and "Nope, never heard of your company." My favorite was, "Wait... that guy still has a job?" Not exactly the buying signals I was hoping for.

And yet, Jason stood by him. Maybe it was friendship, maybe it was blind faith, maybe it was just startup tunnel vision. Whatever it was, Jason kept trusting Trevor, even as the cracks started to show. Then came the big one: Trevor claimed we were *this close* to getting a major funding round from a well-known tech company. The kind of deal that would put us on the map — and, not coincidentally, justify everyone's lack of salary.

I remember the day Jason found out it was all bullshit. He was in a meeting — one of those meetings — and realized in real time that the entire funding story was fabricated. There was no deal. No check coming. No tech partner. Just lies stacked on lies.

That was the moment. The fork in the road. Jason could've kicked Trevor to the curb, called him out, and saved the rest of us from the fallout. But he didn't. He froze. Maybe it was shame, maybe it was loyalty. But whatever it was, he chose silence. And that silence sank the ship.

Instead of cutting the cancer, Jason let the tumor grow. And it took the whole body down with it — including me. I had left a solid job, taken a risk, and bought into a vision that died not because the product sucked or the team was weak — but because the leader wouldn't lead when it mattered most.

We were collateral damage in a loyalty experiment gone wrong.

LESSON LEARNED

Loyalty is a great quality — until it becomes your excuse for inaction. Jason was a good guy. A smart guy. And I genuinely believe he had the best of intentions. But leadership isn't just about vision and charisma. It's about decisions — especially the hard ones. Especially when they involve people you like.

The truth is, Jason didn't betray me — not directly. But his refusal to stand up, call out the lie, and protect the people who trusted him... that's what did the damage.

As a leader, you have to know when loyalty becomes a liability. There's a fine line between having someone's back and letting them stab everyone else in the front.

So if you ever find yourself leading a team, and you've got a Trevor in your midst — do everyone a favor and show them the door. Fast.

Because once the ship starts sinking, nobody cares how close you were to the guy who drilled the hole.

> Clash of leadership philosophies, generational tension, and the classic "culture fit from hell" scenario.

CHAPTER 12
I KNOW WHAT I'M DOING

Lesson: The wrong job taken for the wrong reasons never leads to the right outcome.

Let's rewind for a second.

After the Jason Fairchild meltdown — you know, the one where his sociopath co-founder torpedoed the company and Jason decided to go down with the ship instead of throwing the anchor overboard — I was suddenly unemployed.

Fired. Out. Thank you for playing.

And like most people in that position, I didn't do what I should've done: pause, reflect, figure out what mattered next. Nope. I did what most people do when the mortgage is looming and the career confidence is in the toilet — I jumped at the next opportunity that looked even remotely stable.

That's how I ended up at a company selling technology to Head Start programs.

Now let me say this: the mission was admirable. Truly. Helping early childhood education providers serve their communities better through software? Amazing. The product had a purpose. The customers were doing good in the world. It should have been a place I could thrive.

But the truth is, I didn't look closely enough — not at the culture, not at the leadership, and definitely not at the people I'd be managing.

Also, let's be real: the pay wasn't great. I told myself it was temporary. "Just get back on your feet," I said. "You can turn this into something." Spoiler: I couldn't.

From day one, it was clear I was walking into a setup. I was given a team — a junior sales squad — that had previously been led by Linda Bloom, the head of sales. Linda was... let's say maternal, in the way that kindergarten teachers are maternal. The team had been raised on yeses. They'd been conditioned to think that success was defined by effort, not outcomes. And Linda? She liked it that way. She wanted harmony, not hustle.

Then I showed up.

I wanted accountability, structure, results. I believed in pushing people to be better — not just to make more calls, but to grow, to take ownership, to learn how to work. That's what I thought leaders were supposed to do. That's what I wanted someone to do for me when I was just starting out.

But these reps weren't having it. They saw me as the strict stepdad who moved in and turned off the Wi-Fi. And every time I tried to hold the line — every time I asked them to dig a little deeper, push a little harder, act like professionals — they ran straight to Linda.

And Linda? She gave them whatever they needed. Comfort. Excuses. Validation. And a big ol' smile that said, "Don't worry, I know what I'm doing."

Except... she didn't.

The senior sales team — the people actually closing deals and driving revenue — didn't take a single cue from Linda. They operated like a separate company. They got results because they knew what they were doing and didn't rely on "vibe checks" or pep talks to stay motivated. Meanwhile, the junior team drifted further into underperformance, and the culture started to feel more like a daycare than a sales floor.

Eventually, it came to a head. The company had to choose between the warm hug of Linda's leadership style and the uncomfortable pressure of mine.

Guess who got the axe?

Yep. I was out. Again.

But this time, it wasn't a surprise. I saw it coming the moment I realized performance was optional and criticism was treated like harassment.

LESSON LEARNED

This chapter wasn't about learning that Linda didn't know what she was doing. It was about learning that I didn't know what I was walking into — and I didn't stop to find out.

I took a job for the paycheck and the ego boost of having a team — without asking if it was the right fit for me. I thought I could change the culture. What I didn't realize was that I was the outsider, trying to implement structure in a system designed to avoid it. And Linda? She didn't need to change. She had what she wanted: control without responsibility, popularity without pressure.

So here's the real lesson: Don't take a job just to get back on the horse. Don't jump at the first lifeboat after a shipwreck. And for the love of all that's holy, don't manage a team that doesn't want to be managed.

I learned that I need challenge, grit, accountability. I don't thrive in environments where feedback is seen as mean and growth feels optional. And honestly, I'd rather get fired for pushing too hard than stay employed for coasting too soft.

Sometimes the job you can do is not the job you should do.

Thanks for the lesson, Linda.

(And I still don't believe you knew what you were doing.)

INTERLUDE
LOOKING FOR A CAREER, NOT A JOB

Lesson: Sometimes the best career move is doing absolutely nothing… for a minute.

After the Linda Bloom situation went up in flames (see previous chapter for full meltdown), I was unemployed — again. Two jobs. Two firings. Two wildly different leadership disasters. One common denominator? Me.

Now let me clarify — I don't mean that I was the *problem*. But I finally realized that I'd been reacting, not choosing. Saying "yes" to the next thing because it was available, not because it was *right*. And that's how you end up in companies where the Kool-Aid is mandatory, the meetings are therapy sessions, and somehow being "accountable" is considered a toxic trait.

So, I did something radical:
I hit pause.

No résumé blitz. No "I'll take anything that pays" mindset. No panic-apply-to-100-LinkedIn-postings-in-your-pajamas routine. Instead, I asked myself a question that, frankly, should've come a decade earlier:

Who do I want to be when I grow up?
(Yes, I was already grown up. That's what made it worse.)

And not just what *title* I wanted — what kind of leader, teammate, person I wanted to be professionally. I thought back on every chapter of my career so far: the good, the bad, and the very sweaty (see: fixing toilets). And I realized something simple but powerful:

I don't want to work with assholes.

That became Rule #1.

It turns out, I'm not the only one who feels this way. There's an actual book called *The No Asshole Rule* by Robert Sutton — and yes, that's the real title, and yes, it's as amazing as it sounds. The core idea? One toxic person can ruin an entire culture. Preach, Professor Sutton.

I started thinking about what mattered to me:

- Respect, both given and earned.
- A culture where you can challenge each other *without* having to write a follow-up Slack message explaining your tone.
- A team that likes to win, but doesn't need to burn people out to get there.
- Leaders who lead, not just talk about leadership on LinkedIn.
- And fun. Yes, fun. If we can't laugh a little during the grind, what's the damn point?

So instead of looking for *a job*, I started looking for *a fit*. And the difference was night and day. I didn't want just another paycheck. I wanted purpose, progress, and people who made me better — and let me make them better, too.

I didn't know where I'd end up next, but for the first time, I knew how to evaluate it. I knew how to ask better questions. And more importantly, I knew how to *walk away* from something that wasn't right — even if the money looked good, even if the perks were shiny, even if it meant sitting in the discomfort a little longer.

LESSON LEARNED

Careers aren't built by constantly sprinting to the next opportunity. They're shaped by the moments when you stop, zoom out, and *decide* who you want to be — not just what you want to do.

After Linda, I stopped chasing jobs and started pursuing alignment. I started trusting that short-term discomfort is better than long-term resentment. And I learned that "culture fit" isn't about ping-pong tables and casual Fridays — it's about whether you can be *you* and still thrive.

So if you've been job-hopping, or just taking the next thing that comes along, stop. Ask yourself:

Am I building a career, or just collecting paychecks between breakdowns?

Your answer might change your entire trajectory. Mine definitely did.

PART III
TRANSFORMATION & LEADERSHIP

> Sometimes the hardest hits come from the people who once clapped the loudest.

CHAPTER 13
GREAT TO BLAME

It started out as one of those rare career moments where everything *just felt right*. The people, the culture, the mission — hell, even the sketchy carpet in the office felt like it had potential. I joined Small Footprint when it was a scrappy little team of four of us in a modest U.S. office, paired with a team of twenty folks overseas. There wasn't a lot of polish, but there was something better: fit.

Richard, the CEO, was sharp, driven, and for all intents and purposes, seemed like the kind of guy you could build something great with. I was brought on as part of the executive team, responsible for sales — which, at that point, meant everything from finding new logos to figuring out how to make the coffee machine work without blowing a fuse. It wasn't glamorous, but it was exciting. I even took a pay cut to join, because I believed in the vision. That's how strong the fit felt.

And we *did* build something great. Over the next seven and a half years, we grew the business by 500%. The deals got bigger, the clients got more complex, and slowly but surely, that tiny team with twenty overseas engineers and a handful of desk chairs in the U.S. became a legit contender. I poured myself into it. This wasn't just a job — it was a chapter of my life I genuinely loved.

But here's the thing they don't tell you when you help build something: the bigger it gets, the less control you have.

As we grew, so did the pressure. More revenue, more process, more politics. Richard and his partner started thinking about a sale. And while that made sense from a business perspective, it started to shift the dynamic. Decisions weren't about long-term vision anymore — they were about optics, positioning, and lining things up for acquisition.

Enter: the snake.

I hired a guy. On paper, he was great — background in sales, smooth talker, claimed to have all the right connections. In reality, he was a professional ass-kisser. But not the harmless kind — the *strategic* kind. The kind who made friends in high places by throwing people under the bus in the hallway. He figured out quickly that Richard wanted validation, and he served it up like a buffet.

And here's where I made the mistake: I didn't play that game. I never have. I don't politic. I don't suck up. I figured the years of loyalty, the numbers I delivered, and the trust we'd built would speak louder than this guy's flattery. I figured wrong.

When he started screwing up, I assumed it would be obvious. He wasn't closing deals, wasn't delivering value, and worse — he was eroding trust within the team. But instead of seeing that, Richard started listening to him. And when fingers started pointing, guess who they landed on?

Me. The guy who'd helped build the sales engine from the ground up. The one who worked through every stage of growth. Suddenly, I wasn't a founding partner — I was a liability.

It's a surreal feeling to go from core team member to outsider in a place you helped build. I could feel it shift. The meetings I used to lead, I was now barely invited to. My input was "noted" instead of valued. And eventually, Richard made me an offer to buy me out before the company sold.

On paper, it was clean. Professional. On the surface, people called it a "transition." But inside, it wrecked me. I felt betrayed. I'd given years of my life to this company. I'd turned down more money elsewhere. I'd believed in the mission — and in Richard.

And now? I was out. Not because I failed. But because I didn't flatter the right people.

It changed something in me. I started to believe that the longer you're somewhere, the more vulnerable you are. The more you succeed, the more you have to protect. And the more you trust, the harder it hurts when that trust is broken.

To this day, Small Footprint is one of the companies I loved the most — and the one that hurt the most when it ended.

LESSON LEARNED

This one hurt. Not because I lost a job — I've lost jobs before — but because I lost trust. I learned the hard way that as companies grow, politics grow too, and the relationships that carried you at the start don't always protect you in the end. It taught me to pay closer attention to culture shifts, to spot the warning signs when loyalty starts getting traded for optics, and to guard against letting someone else's agenda define my value. The hardest part wasn't being blamed; it was realizing I had trusted someone who didn't deserve it — and that I'd let them through the door myself.

CHAPTER 13 UPDATE – FOUR YEARS LATER

Time has a funny way of softening sharp edges.

About four years after the company sold — long after the bitterness had cooled and the sting of being pushed out had dulled — Richard and I reconnected. No big dramatic movie moment, no tearful reunion in the rain. Just two people who'd been through something big together, finally ready to talk about it without the baggage.

We both owned our part in how it ended. He admitted there were things he would've done differently. I admitted I probably could've handled things better too (don't tell him I said that). There wasn't a winner or loser in that conversation — just two guys who'd built something they loved, watching it play out in ways neither of us expected.

Today, we're friends again. We can laugh about it now — even if I still give him hell for selling the one company I thought I could ride into retirement. ("Seriously, Richard, you couldn't wait just ten more years?") He laughs, I laugh, and we both know that, for better or worse, Small Footprint will always be one of the most defining chapters in both our careers.

> Sometimes you don't need to fight harder – you just need backup.

CHAPTER 14
KNOW WHEN TO BRING IN THE CAVALRY

Every salesperson has "that" account — the one you chase for years, the one that turns into your personal Everest. For me, at Small Footprint, that account was Frank Donnelly.

Frank was the kind of customer you wanted in your corner: smart, straightforward, and — most importantly — a die-hard Giants fan. Which, as anyone who's spent time in sales knows, is half the battle. You find that one thing you can connect on — sports, kids, mutual hatred of the Cowboys — and suddenly the door cracks open.

With Frank, it took three years to get through that door. Three years of emails, calls, and trips to his city where I would take him out for drinks (lots of drinks) and, occasionally, what we liked to call the "urban ballet" — also known as a night at the local strip club. (Don't judge. Sometimes business relationships are built on fancy dinners. Other times, they're built on shared awkward glances at questionable dance routines.)

Eventually, all that persistence paid off. Frank became a customer. And not just any customer — a big one. The kind of account that made you look good on the executive dashboard. We did good work for him, and the relationship felt solid. We'd talk Giants football, grab drinks when we were in the same city, and I genuinely liked the guy.

But here's the thing about good relationships: they're fragile. And mine with Frank was about to crack.

After our first year working together, I sent him a renewal quote. In hindsight, I underpriced it. I'd given him a sweetheart deal without thinking about how it might look internally. When Richard — the CEO, and this was during our "rough patch" — saw the quote, he told me to rescind it. Raise the price.

I knew it was going to tick Frank off, but I did what I was told. I called him, explained the change, and tried to smooth it over. It did not go well. Frank was furious — not just about the price hike, but about the fact that Richard never came to see him. "We're a big customer," he said. "Where's your CEO?"

And that's when I made my mistake.

Instead of pulling Richard in — instead of saying, "Hey, this is getting bigger than me; I need help" — I tried to handle it myself. I figured I'd built the relationship, I could fix it. I didn't want to look weak. I didn't want to admit I needed backup. So I kept grinding, sending emails, calling, meeting Frank in person, thinking I could patch it over with enough hustle.

It didn't work.

Frank stayed upset. The account cooled. And looking back, I realized it didn't have to play out that way. Richard showing up might not have fixed everything, but it would have shown Frank we valued him at the highest level. Sometimes the "ask for help" moment isn't about saving you — it's about showing the customer they matter enough to bring in the cavalry.

LESSON LEARNED

This chapter taught me something I wish I'd learned earlier in my career: knowing when to ask for help isn't weakness — it's strategy. I thought protecting the relationship meant keeping it all on my shoulders, but that just left me alone when things got tough. If I'd pulled Richard in sooner, Frank would've seen a company that cared, not just a salesman scrambling. In leadership and sales, there's a balance: do what you can yourself, but recognize when the moment calls for backup. Sometimes the most powerful thing you can do is raise your hand and say, "I need you on this one."

It's all fun and games until someone asks you to recite your own values.

CHAPTER 15
BETTER KNOW YOUR COMPANY VALUES

There are cool people. And then there are people who make "cool" look like an understatement. Tim Wolf was firmly in the second category.

Tim was an engineering leader at a fast-moving startup in Charleston — the kind of guy who could lead a stand-up with one hand and shoot an alligator between the eyes with the other. And that's not hyperbole. Tim actually hunted alligators. With a bow and arrow. He had stories about it that he'd tell over beers or while we bowled — casual, like other people talk about golf. I was impressed and slightly terrified at the same time.

But what really stood out about Tim wasn't just the alligator thing (although, come on — how do you top that?). It was how he built his teams. The guy was magnetic. He attracted smart people, built them into cohesive units, and created a culture that made them want to run through walls for him. And the secret sauce? He actually believed in the company's values. Not the laminated-poster kind. The lived-out, woven-into-every-decision kind.

I learned that the hard way.

One day, Tim, me, and one of my fellow executives were in a meeting with him. We were talking about collaboration, about how we needed better alignment between our teams, when Tim suddenly stopped and asked:

"Hey, can you name your company values?"

I froze. My exec froze. We looked at each other like two kids who'd been called on in class without doing the reading. Because the truth was... we couldn't. We didn't know them.

Tim didn't gloat. He didn't need to. The silence said everything. Here we were, talking about building culture, selling vision, driving alignment — and we couldn't even name the values we were supposedly championing. It was embarrassing. More than that, it was a wake-up call.

Because Tim *knew* his company's values. He could recite them, sure — but more importantly, he lived them. Every decision, every hire, every project — he filtered it all through those values. And he expected the same from everyone around him. If you didn't know yours, how could you possibly expect your teams to buy in?

We stayed friends after that meeting. Kept bowling, kept drinking beer, kept swapping ridiculous alligator stories. But that moment stuck with me. It changed how I thought about culture. It's not enough to plaster values on a wall or drop them in a slide deck. People can smell when it's just for show. The real test? Can you recite them? Can you live them? Can you prove it when someone like Tim Wolf calls you out in the middle of a meeting?

LESSON LEARNED

Tim taught me that culture isn't a slogan — it's a standard. Company values only matter if they're baked into how you hire, lead, and make decisions. If you can't name them, you can't live them. And if you don't live them, your team won't either. That moment — sitting there, blank-faced, unable to answer Tim's question — forced me to reevaluate not just what I believed, but how I practiced it. Now, whether I'm building a team or joining one, I make sure I know the values by heart — and more importantly, that I actually believe them. Because if you don't believe them, neither will anyone else.

> Sometimes the next step isn't a promotion – it's a leap off a cliff.

CHAPTER 16
WTF AM I THINKING!

When Small Footprint sold, I felt unmoored. I wasn't excited about the new ownership, and for the first time in a while, I didn't know what was next. I took a stopgap role at another similar company — a paycheck, nothing more — and while it paid the bills, it didn't feed anything else. I was restless.

Then Caroline Mercer called.

Caroline had been a customer back in my Small Footprint days, and she was now leading technology at Riverstone Health — a massive healthcare system with more complexity than anything I'd ever touched. We hadn't talked in a while, but she didn't waste time catching up.

"Come work for me," she said. "Run a division for me."

My immediate thought? WTF am I thinking?

This wasn't sales. It wasn't familiar. It wasn't even close to the lane I'd been driving in for years. This was leading a division that sold, implemented, and supported a healthcare system for private practices partnering with Riverstone. There were no processes in place. No roadmap. I'd have to build everything from scratch while leading people through major change.

And I didn't have a clue how to do it.

But Caroline did. Or at least, she believed I could figure it out. She saw something in me I wasn't sure I saw in myself yet. She told me to lean into the fear, to treat it like fuel instead of a warning sign.

That's when I stumbled onto *Mindset* by Dr. Carol Dweck. The book broke it down simply: fixed mindset vs. growth mindset. Fixed says "I can't." Growth says "I can learn." Fixed says "Stay where it's safe." Growth says "Do the scary thing."

I realized I'd been operating out of fear — not because I couldn't do the work, but because I was afraid of failing at something new. Caroline's encouragement and that book flipped the script. Suddenly, I was asking myself: What if fear is exactly where I need to go?

So I jumped.

And it was hard — every bit as hard as I imagined. I walked into an environment where the playbook didn't exist. I had to build process, create structure, and drive massive change management in a space I barely understood. The learning curve was steep, but I leaned on what I did know — leading teams, listening, connecting, and adapting fast. Over time, the chaos started to make sense. The division grew. We accomplished things no one thought possible when I first walked in the door.

Would I have taken that leap without Caroline's push? Probably not. But it changed the trajectory of my career — and it changed how I approach fear.

LESSON LEARNED

Before this, I thought career growth meant climbing a straight ladder — getting better at what you already know. This role taught me something different: real growth is diagonal. It happens when you step sideways into something unknown and trust yourself to figure it out.

Caroline showed me the power of someone else believing in you before you believe in yourself. And *Mindset* gave me the framework to lean into fear instead of letting it paralyze me. Building that division forced me to develop new muscles — process design, change management, leading in ambiguity — that made me a better leader everywhere I've gone since.

The takeaway? Fear is a compass. If something scares you but also excites you, that's probably the thing you need to do. And if you're lucky, you'll have someone like Caroline in your corner, giving you the nudge you didn't know you needed.

> Sometimes culture isn't one big thing – it's a thousand little ones stacked together.

CHAPTER 17
MICRO WHAT?! THAT'S WHAT SHE SAID...

When I landed at Riverstone Health, I walked straight into chaos. Not bad chaos — just the kind that happens when an organization is shifting from old ways of working to something completely new. My job? Lead my division through that shift.

We weren't just changing tools or tweaking processes. We were rewiring how the team thought about work. We were moving from traditional project management to agile methodology and product thinking — two phrases that sound simple in theory and feel like learning a foreign language in practice.

I brought in an old colleague to help because I knew this wasn't something I could do alone. Together, we rolled out new frameworks, coached the teams through sprints and stand-ups, and rebuilt how they planned, delivered, and iterated. It was messy at first — change always is — but eventually, something clicked. The team embraced the new way of working, and the results spoke for themselves. We were moving faster, collaborating better, and delivering more value than we ever had before.

I was proud. Really proud.

Then along came Misti Fragen.

Misti worked in organizational change and transformation — think culture audits, communications strategies, and those "listening tours" where someone shows up and asks everyone what's working and what isn't. Caroline had tasked her with reviewing how the broader Digital Product organization was handling the agile transition, and naturally, that included my team.

Now, I'll admit: I was nervous. "Review" is one of those words that can either mean "tell us how awesome we are" or "find out why everything's broken." But Misti's approach wasn't about blame. She wanted to understand.

When she finished her listening tour, she surprised me.

"Your team," she said, "is the only one that's actually made this work."

I should have felt vindicated — and I did — but Misti wasn't there to hand out gold stars. She was there to ask the next question: *Why is your team succeeding where others aren't?*

That's where she introduced me to the idea of macro and micro culture.

Every company, she explained, has a macro culture — the overarching values, norms, and way of working that defines the organization. But within that, every team creates its own micro culture — the day-to-day behaviors, rituals, and dynamics that make them unique.

The mistake most leaders make? Pretending culture is one-size-fits-all.

Misti helped me see that my team's success wasn't just because we'd implemented agile well. It was because we'd built a micro culture that worked for us — one that aligned with Riverstone's overall values but gave us the flexibility to operate in our own way. We weren't fighting the macro culture; we were complementing it.

That realization was a game changer. It gave me permission to stop obsessing over whether every other team worked like mine — and to start focusing on building the best possible micro culture for the people I led.

LESSON LEARNED

Before Misti, I thought culture was something you set at the top and handed down like commandments. She taught me it's more layered than that — every organization has a big-picture culture (macro) and countless subcultures (micro) that form around teams, leaders, and even projects. The trick isn't forcing everyone into one mold; it's making sure those micro cultures align with the macro values while letting teams find their own rhythm.

That insight changed how I lead. Instead of obsessing over uniformity, I focus on alignment. Are we living the company's core values? Yes? Great. Now how do we make *this team*'s culture something people want to be part of? It's like agile itself — flexible, adaptable, and never truly "done."

> Sometimes the ones who cheer you on the loudest are also the first to step aside when it matters most.

CHAPTER 18
THE WOLF IN KHAKIS AND AN OXFORD

By the time I took my second product leadership role, I thought I'd seen it all — messy teams, chaotic processes, leaders who wanted transformation but panicked when they actually got it. But nothing prepared me for this one.

The company was in pharmaceuticals and CPG, and I was responsible for products that made up 55–60% of total revenue. Let me repeat that: more than half of the company's revenue. It was both exhilarating and terrifying — like being handed the keys to a race car while someone whispered, "Oh, by the way, the brakes are iffy."

This was another transformation gig, which was quickly becoming my specialty. The teams were siloed; product management processes were either nonexistent or ignored, and sales and operations were basically playing two different sports. My job? Un-silo everyone, implement product thinking, and somehow convince the entire company — including executives — that this was not just "nice to have," but critical for survival.

When I came in, I reported to the division president, Martin Keene. Martin was a decent guy and basically told me, Do what you have to do. Fix it.

What he didn't realize — and what I learned fast — was just how broken things really were.

- Processes? Broken.
- Culture? Fractured.
- Communication? Nonexistent.
- The upside? There was nowhere to go but up.

So I started with quick wins. I found pain points, fixed them fast, and earned trust. Slowly, we got the basics in place — real product roadmaps, cross-team collaboration, agile processes that didn't just exist on paper. Then came the hard part: changing mindsets. Getting people — especially sales and operations — to stop clinging to old ways and actually buy into the new approach.

And that's when the musical chairs of leadership began.

First, the CEO "retired." Then my boss, Martin, "retired." (I use quotes because these weren't "gold watch and cake" retirements — more like "we'll say retired so nobody panics" retirements.) Suddenly, I was reporting to Carla Micromantra, the new president of the division.

Carla… how do I put this delicately? She was not Martin. She knew less about process than Martin — which is saying something — and yet wanted her hands in everything. Nothing slows down transformation like someone micromanaging what they don't understand. We made progress, but it felt like pushing a boulder uphill while someone kept adding bricks to it.

And then, just as suddenly as she arrived, Carla was gone. Boss number three: Jonathan Vance, the new CEO.

Jonathan felt different right away. He was sharp, charismatic, and understood what I was trying to do. When I vented to him about my frustrations with Carla, he didn't dismiss me. He listened. He validated. He even said something that stuck with me:

"Hold on. Help is coming."

We talked about mental health — something close to me because of my sister — and how leadership needs to do more to support people, not just profits. I left those conversations believing he had my back. I thought, *Finally. Someone who gets it.*

Spoiler alert: he didn't.

Enter boss number four in two years: a new SVP, brought in by Jonathan. And this guy wanted his own team. Which meant I was out.

What stung wasn't just losing the role. It was realizing Jonathan — and even Eddie Callahan, the CFO, who I knew personally from past work and shared fandom for the same college team — didn't fight for me. These were people who had encouraged me, told me to keep "fighting the fight," praised the transformation we'd achieved... and when the knives came out, they went quiet.

It was a gut punch. Because up until then, I'd believed in the myth that if you did good work, if you stayed loyal, if you kept your head down and delivered — leadership would have your back. This experience shattered that myth.

I got fooled again — this time at the highest level.

LESSON LEARNED

Jonathan and Eddie taught me one of the hardest lessons of my career: words are cheap when they aren't backed up by action. They cheered me on, encouraged me to push for transformation, and promised their support — but when it came time to prove it, they disappeared.

This is how I lead: I refuse to give hollow encouragement. If I tell someone I've got their back, I mean it. And if I can't support them, I won't pretend I can. Because nothing erodes trust faster than leaders who talk about loyalty but go silent when it's tested.

I also learned this: no matter how high up you go, politics doesn't disappear. The stakes just get bigger, and the fallout hurts more. That doesn't mean stop trusting — but it does mean trust with your eyes open.

PART IV
HONORING THE MENTORS

> Some lessons find you by accident.
> Others you have to go out and ask for.

CHAPTER 19
HOMAGE TO MY INTENTIONAL MENTORS

I've spent this entire book talking about unintentional mentors — the bosses who taught me what *not* to do, the co-workers who unknowingly shaped me, the people who accidentally left me better (or tougher) than they found me. But if I ended the book there, it would be incomplete.

Because some of the most important lessons I've learned didn't come by accident — they came because I asked for them.

Over the last decade, I've been lucky enough to have four incredible intentional mentors. These are people I didn't just cross paths with; I deliberately sought them out. I chose each of them for a very specific reason — one area where I wanted to grow — and approached them using the framework I created and call the 15 Minute Mentor. (I'll explain the framework itself at the end of this book, but the short version: choose one mentor, one topic, and one clear goal. Keep it focused, keep it intentional.)

These four people — Michael, Earl, Dean, and Charles — have shaped me in ways no single boss or job ever could. Here's what I've learned from each of them.

MICHAEL SMITH – CULTURE AND BRANDING IT

I met Michael Smith about nine years ago when he was the CIO at Estée Lauder. You know how some people walk into a room and instantly make it feel calm? That's Michael. He's thoughtful, unflappable, and somehow manages to make "building culture" feel less like an HR buzzword and more like a leadership superpower.

I'd worked with plenty of people who could talk about culture — plaster values on walls, put them in slide decks — but Michael *lived* it. You could feel it in how his teams operated. They didn't just know the values; they embodied them. That's what I wanted to learn from him: not just how to *set* a culture, but how to brand it, live it, and make it stick.

Our conversations changed the way I approach leadership. Michael taught me that culture is a promise. If you tell your team you value transparency, you'd better prove it when things go sideways. If you say you value growth, you'd better invest in it when budgets get tight. Culture isn't what you write down — it's what people see you do when it's inconvenient.

Outside of mentoring, Michael and I have become close friends. Along with Earl, another good friend (more on him in a second), we co-founded TechPACT, an organization built on the belief that anyone who wants to succeed in technology should have that opportunity. And because I apparently can't just have normal friendships, I have a part ownership, although small, in a Northern Ireland soccer team that Micahel owns — the Carrick Rangers. If that sounds random, it is. But that's what happens when you mix business conversations with pints and good timing.

EARL NEWSOME – THOUGHT LEADERSHIP

I met Earl around the same time I met Michael. At the time, Earl was carving out a reputation as one of the most forward-thinking CIOs in the industry, and he remains one of the best storytellers I've ever known. The man could pitch a vision for IT modernization and make it sound like you were signing up for an adventure, not a project plan.

We officially met over steak at Wolfgang's in New York. I introduced Earl to Michael that night, and in the process, I also introduced both of them to a drink called "The Seth" (Don't ask what's in it — just know it involves vodka), and the proper way to drink Sambuca, yes, you have to have three coffee beans floating in it. Non-negotiable.

Earl became my mentor for thought leadership. Specifically: how do you get people to buy into your ideas — not just understand them, but *believe* in them? Earl's gift is taking something complex, framing it with a compelling narrative, and tying it back to why it matters.

From Earl, I learned that thought leadership isn't about being the loudest voice — it's about being the clearest. It's about connecting dots other people can't see and telling the story in a way that makes them say, "Of course. That's obvious. Why aren't we already doing this?"

DEAN DEL VECCHIO – EXECUTIVE BUY-IN

Dean is proof that sometimes your best mentors show up in unexpected places — like the beach. Our families have neighboring beach houses in New Jersey, and I met him in passing while he was the CIO/COO at Guardian Life.

Dean's gift — the thing I asked him to mentor me on — is getting executive leadership on board. He's brilliant at helping executives understand *why* a change matters, not just *what* the change is. And as someone who has spent most of my career driving transformation, I needed that skill. Badly.

I used to think getting buy-in meant explaining the benefits. Dean showed me it's about understanding the fears. What's the risk your change introduces? What's the comfort it threatens? If you don't address those things first, your pitch — no matter how logical — will fall flat.

Dean also taught me that getting buy-in isn't a one-time event. It's ongoing. You don't just sell the vision once; you reinforce it constantly, especially when the road gets bumpy. That approach has saved me more than once in the years since.

CHARLES GRESSLE – TRUE LEADERSHIP

Charles and I go way back — all the way to MBA school, where we were classmates. Watching someone you studied alongside rise to become President of HCA East Florida has been both humbling and inspiring. Charles proves that peers can be mentors, too.

Charles is one of the most relentlessly positive leaders I know. And not in a cheesy, "good vibes only" kind of way — in a grounded, "I know this is hard, but we're going to figure it out together" kind of way. That positivity isn't fluff; it's fuel. It aligns his teams to his vision and gives them the courage to chase it.

When I asked Charles to mentor me, it wasn't about strategy or process. It was about mindset. How do you keep people motivated when things get hard? How do you align a team around a vision without forcing it? Charles's answer: live it yourself. If you want your team to stay optimistic, you have to model optimism. If you want them to trust you, you have to trust them first.

LESSON LEARNED

These four mentors remind me why intentional mentorship matters. Unintentional mentors teach you through observation — often by accident. Intentional mentors teach you because you ask them to. They give you access to wisdom you might never stumble onto yourself.

The 15 Minute Mentor approach — choosing one mentor for one topic at a time — has been my way of making those relationships focused and respectful. And it works. Michael taught me how to brand and live culture. Earl taught me how to craft vision into story. Dean taught me how to win hearts and minds at the executive table. Charles taught me how to lead with positivity that's real, not performative.

Each of them added a piece to my leadership puzzle. And together, they've shaped the leader I am — and the leader I'm still becoming.

> Sometimes the people who shape you most don't even know you exist.

CHAPTER 20
UNINTENTIONAL MENTORS I NEVER MET, BUT HOPE TO

I've spent this book talking about the people I've worked with — the good, the bad, the ones who yelled across bars, and the ones who co-owned soccer teams with me. But there's another group of mentors who have shaped me just as much: the ones I've never met.

Books have always been part of my leadership journey. Not in a "sit by the fire and read classics" way — more like "panic-read a chapter at 2 a.m. before a big presentation" way. Certain authors have a knack for saying exactly what I need to hear at exactly the right moment. These three — Patrick Lencioni, Melissa Perri, and Robert I. Sutton — are basically the Mount Rushmore of my unintentional mentors. I've never shaken their hands, but they've had a bigger impact on me than some people I've shared offices with.

PATRICK LENCIONI – THE MAN CRUSH

Let's get this out of the way: I have a full-on man crush on Patrick Lencioni. There, I said it.

I first stumbled on his work at Small Footprint when someone handed me *The Five Dysfunctions of a Team*. At the time, I thought I had a pretty good handle on team dynamics. Spoiler: I didn't. Patrick's book broke it down in a way that felt both obvious and life-changing. He made me realize that trust isn't just "nice to have" — it's the foundation everything else rests on. No trust, no team.

From there, I devoured everything he wrote. *The Ideal Team Player. Getting Naked* (not what it sounds like, but still a great way to freak out coworkers when they see the title on your desk). And later, his *Working Genius* framework, which has become one of my favorite tools for helping teams figure out not just what they do, but what energizes them.

Patrick talks about things that are deceptively simple — so simple you almost feel dumb for not thinking of them yourself. But that's the magic. He reminds you of the fundamentals in a way that makes you actually use them. During COVID, I even started listening to his podcast on runs. There's something comforting about hearing him talk through team challenges while you're gasping for air and wondering why you thought running was a good idea in the first place.

MELISSA PERRI – THE SCHOOL BOY

If Patrick is the man crush, Melissa Perri is the product crush.

Melissa is widely considered one of the leading voices in product management — especially around Product Operations. For someone like me, who's spent years building product teams and processes, her work has been a revelation.

I remember reading her book, *Escaping the Build Trap*, and thinking, *Oh, so this is what I've been trying to do — but she actually put words to it.* She broke down the difference between building features and delivering real outcomes in a way that made me completely rethink how I approached product strategy.

The ultimate fan-boy moment? I messaged her on LinkedIn one Saturday morning with a random question. Not only did she respond — she actually went back and forth with me for a bit. Do you understand what that does to someone who quotes her frameworks in meetings to sound smart? I might as well have been a teenager getting a text from their favorite rock star.

Even though I never landed the product ops role I interviewed for, her frameworks still influence how I work today. And honestly, being able to drop her name in conversations has earned me more "cred" than I probably deserve.

ROBERT I. SUTTON – THE BIBLE

Then there's Robert Sutton, who wrote what I lovingly refer to as "my bible": *The No Asshole Rule.*

I found this book right before I interviewed at Small Footprint. I was so hooked I actually handed a copy to Richard — yes, during the interview process. Probably not your standard interview etiquette, but hey, it worked.

Sutton's message is simple: don't work with assholes. Don't hire them. Don't tolerate them. Don't let them ruin your culture. And if you *are* one, fix it or get out. It sounds obvious, but I can't tell you how many companies ignore this — and pay for it later.

This book gave me language for something I'd felt my whole career: one bad apple really can spoil the bunch. Protect your team from toxic people, no matter how talented they are. It's not just about avoiding pain — it's about creating space for everyone else to thrive.

To this day, I recommend *The No Asshole Rule* more than any other leadership book. I quote it in meetings. I've gifted it to friends. It's basically required reading for anyone who works with me.

LESSON LEARNED

These three authors have shaped my leadership philosophy in ways that rival any boss I've had. Patrick taught me that simplicity and trust are the foundation of any great team. Melissa showed me how product management — and operations — can drive real outcomes instead of empty outputs. And Sutton? He reminded me that culture is worth defending, even if it means walking away from talent that doesn't fit.

They're unintentional mentors — people I've never met but feel like I know. Their books have been my late-night coaches, my sounding boards on long runs, and my secret weapons in countless leadership conversations. And while I'd love to meet them someday, I'm grateful for what I've learned even from afar. Sometimes the best mentors are the ones who don't even know they're doing it.

> The story doesn't really end here –
> it just changes chapters.

CHAPTER 21
WHAT IS TO COME

If you've made it this far, you've heard a lot of stories about the people who shaped me — the unintentional mentors who didn't know they were teaching me, and the intentional ones I sought out because I knew I needed them. You've seen the good, the bad, the assholes, and the legends. You've heard about my failures and the occasional win. And somehow, all of it led me here.

Right now, I'm the Chief Growth Officer at Tricon. That title still feels weird to say out loud. It sounds big, official, like I should have a private jet or at least an assistant who brings me sparkling water with lime. (Spoiler: I don't.) What I do have is a seat at the table where big decisions get made — and the chance to put everything I've learned into practice, every single day.

But here's the thing: I'm still learning.

The funny part about leadership is that the higher you go, the less certain you feel. You think you'll get to a point where you "arrive," where the questions stop and the answers come easy. Instead, you realize leadership is just one long series of new questions. Every promotion, every new challenge, every new team — it's another chance to get humbled, to adapt, to grow.

The lessons from my unintentional mentors? They're with me every time I decide to push through fear, every time I spot politics creeping in, every time I remind myself not to become the kind of leader I swore I'd never be.

The lessons from my intentional mentors? They're in how I build culture, how I tell stories, how I align people to vision without forcing it.

And maybe — just maybe — I'm someone else's unintentional mentor now. Maybe there's someone on my team who's watching how I handle a tough conversation, or how I show up in a crisis, or how I admit when I screw up. Maybe one day they'll write their own version of this book and I'll be in it — either as a leader who inspired them... or as the cautionary tale they never want to repeat. (Honestly? I hope for the first one. But hey, I know how this works.)

I don't know exactly what's next. I know I'll keep making mistakes. I know I'll keep trying to learn from them. And I know I'll keep leaning on the lessons — intentional and unintentional — that got me this far.

If there's one thing this journey has taught me, it's that growth isn't a destination. It's a habit. And as long as I keep that habit alive, I like where this story is headed.

LESSON LEARNED

The story isn't about "arriving." It's about staying curious, staying humble, and staying open to the mentors you don't even realize are shaping you. The next chapter of my career will be built on everything I've learned so far — and everything I haven't learned yet. Because growth, it turns out, never really stops.

BONUS CHAPTER
THE 15 MINUTE MENTOR FRAMEWORK (YOURS FREE!)

So... what now?

This whole book has been about learning from the people around you, but growth doesn't stop when you finish the last chapter. It's not like, *Great, I'm cured!* No — leadership is a lifelong work-in-progress. Which is why I want to give you something practical to use going forward: the exact framework I use to keep learning from mentors even when everyone is "too busy."

I call it the 15 Minute Mentor Framework. And you don't even have to pay for it. (Seriously — no ebook upsell, no "buy my course" nonsense. Just take it. It's yours.)

WHERE THE IDEA CAME FROM

I can't take all the credit. The concept was inspired by something I heard on Molly Fletcher's *Game Changers* podcast. Her guest, Gary Keller (yep, the Keller Williams guy), talked about identifying five people who could help you reach your financial goals — and then finding ways to connect with them regularly.

I loved the simplicity of that idea but wanted to apply it to personal growth and leadership. Because I've always had a long list of traits I wanted to work on — patience, storytelling, influencing executives, culture-building — and a long list of incredible people in my network who excel at those exact things. The problem? They're all busy. And I didn't want to waste their time with unfocused "pick your brain" meetings (also known as: "Hey, can I take you to coffee and talk at you for an hour?").

So I tweaked it. I built an approach that's focused, respectful of time, and ridiculously effective.

THE FRAMEWORK

Here's how it works:

1. Pick five traits you want to improve. Not ten. Not seventeen. Five. These are the core things you want to level up in — like storytelling, negotiation, culture, executive presence, or conflict management.

2. Find five mentors — one per trait. Each mentor should represent one thing you want to learn. This does two things: it keeps the ask clear ("I want to get better at *this* and you're great at it") and it prevents overwhelm (no single person has to be your "everything" mentor)

3. Schedule short, recurring meetings. Fifteen minutes. That's it. Monthly, bi-monthly, or quarterly — whatever works for both of you. The point is consistency, not frequency.

4. Follow the agenda. This is where the magic happens. Every 15-minute session runs the same way:
    - First 5 minutes: You update them — what you've done around this trait since your last chat.
    - Next 5 minutes: They give guidance and feedback — what you did well, what you could do differently.
    - Final 5 minutes: Together, you agree on what you'll work on next.

That's it. Fifteen minutes. No rambling. No wasted time. Just focused, high-value mentorship.

WHY IT WORKS

Fifteen minutes might not sound like much, but you'd be shocked at how much progress you can make when you're laser-focused. The short time frame forces you to prepare, prioritize, and actually do the work between sessions. And because the mentors know you're respecting their time, they're more likely to say yes — and to keep saying yes.

Plus, there's something freeing about knowing you don't need one "perfect mentor" to teach you everything. You just need five people willing to teach you *one* thing each. Over time, those five things stack up.

FINAL THOUGHT. REALLY, I SWEAR.

This framework has helped me grow faster than anything else I've tried. It's simple. It's scalable. And it turns mentorship from a vague concept into a concrete habit.

So take it. Use it. Be someone's intentional mentor — or their unintentional one. And when someone asks you years from now how you learned that one leadership move you're known for? Maybe you'll tell them about this little 15-minute thing you read at the end of a book.

ABOUT THE AUTHOR

Seth Carpien is a product and strategy executive who's spent his career helping companies turn chaos into clarity—and data into revenue. He's led teams across industries from tech to healthcare to consumer goods, guiding transformations that stick (and surviving a few that didn't).

Known for his straight talk, dry humor, and obsession with practical leadership, Seth believes the best leaders listen more than they talk, lift others up, and aren't afraid to admit when they've screwed something up.

He's also the co-founder of The Table, a national dinner series that brings tech and product leaders together for real conversations—no sales decks, no buzzwords, just people learning from each other.

When he's not advising companies or writing about leadership gone right (and wrong), you'll probably find him mentoring someone, laughing with friends, or pretending to take notes while thinking about his next story. Unintentional Mentors is his first book.

www.ingramcontent.com/pod-product-compliance
Lightning Source LLC
Chambersburg PA
CBHW030002050426
42451CB00006B/88